Measuring Time

Hours, Minutes, and Seconds

Tracey Steffora

Heinemann Library
Chicago, Illinois

www.heinemannraintree.com
Visit our website to find out more information about Heinemann-Raintree books.

To order:
☎ Phone 888-454-2279
💻 Visit www.heinemannraintree.com to browse our catalog and order online.

Edited by Tracey Steffora and Dan Nunn
Designed by Richard Parker
Picture research by Hannah Taylor
Originated by Capstone Global Library Ltd
Printed and bound in the United States of America,
North Mankato, MN

14 13 12 11
10 9 8 7 6 5 4 3 2

Library of Congress Cataloging-in-Publication Data
Steffora, Tracey.
  Hours, minutes, and seconds / Tracey Steffora.
    p. cm.—(Measuring time)
  Includes bibliographical references and index.
  ISBN 978-1-4329-4900-6 (hc)—ISBN 978-1-4329-4907-5 (pb)
  1. Time—Juvenile literature. 2. Time measurement—Juvenile literature. I. Title.
  QB209.5.S746 2011
  529'.7—dc22
                          2010028825
  062011
  006158RP

Acknowledgments
We would like to thank the following for permission to reproduce photographs: Alamy Images pp. **4** (©OJO Images Ltd), **6** (©John Powell - Photographer), **7** (©Travelscape Images), **12** (©Image Source), **16** (©Juice Images), **20** (©Dave Porter); istockphoto pp. **5** (©Willie B. Thomas), **8** (©Nikada), **9** (©Rich Legg), **10** (©Carmen Martinez Banus), **11** (©Nicolas Loran), **17** (©Sze Kit Poon), **21** (©Christopher Furcher); Photolibrary p. **15** (Hoberman Collection); shutterstock pp. **13** (©Monika Wisniewska), **14** (©zulufoto), **18** (©Tyler Olson), **19** (©Jiri Hera), **23 top** (©Jiri hera), **23 bot** (©Monika Wisniewska).

Front cover photograph of digital clock on station platform reproduced with permission of Getty Images (Jon Bradley). Back cover photograph of people around a cake reproduced with permission of istockphoto (© Rich Legg).

Every effort has been made to contact copyright holders of any material reproduced in this book. Any omissions will be rectified in subsequent printings if notice is given to the publisher.

Contents

What Is Time?

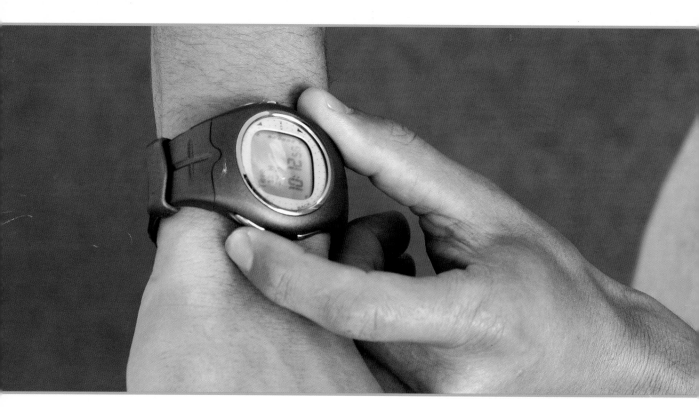

Time is how long something takes.

Some things take a long time.

Some things take a short time.

How Long Is a Second?

A second takes a very short time.

Open your arms wide and clap.

Each clap is about a second.

You can walk across the street
in 10 seconds.

You can sing "Happy Birthday" in 20 seconds.

How Long Is a Minute?

A minute is longer than a second.
There are 60 seconds in 1 minute.

You can wash your hands in one minute.

You can read a book in 10 minutes.

You can wash a load of laundry in 30 minutes.

How Long Is an Hour?

An hour is a lot longer than a minute.

An hour is 60 minutes.

You can play a game of soccer in an hour.

You can bake a loaf of bread in an hour.

There are 24 hours in a day.

A lot can happen in 24 hours!

Clocks

Clocks help us measure time.

The hands on a clock tell us the time.

Using Time

We use time to know when things happen.

Schedule

8:00	Morning Circle
8:30	Reading and Writing
10:00	Snack
10:30	Science
12:00	Lunch
12:30	Recess
1:00	Math
2:00	Art
2:45	Dismissal

We use time to plan our day.

Thinking About Time

60 seconds = 1 minute

60 minutes = 1 hour

24 hours = 1 day

What can you do in a second?

What can you do in a minute?

What can you do in an hour?

Picture Glossary

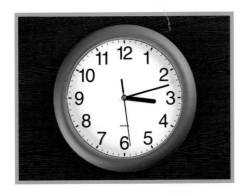

clock something used for measuring and telling the time

laundry clothes that are washed

Index

Note to Parents and Teachers

Before reading

You can help provide children with a sensorial experience of time by having them put their heads down and asking them to raise a hand when they think a minute has passed. Let them know when you begin and end the timing of a minute, and give them several opportunities to predict the length of a minute. If a clock with a second hand is available, gather children around and have them observe one full rotation of the second hand.

After reading

Review the length of a second, a minute, and an hour. With children, discuss and chart examples of things that can be measured in seconds, minutes, or hours.